The Optimum Eight

First Edition

Cover and internal design by Katie McDonnell

Published by Amazon KDP

The Optimum Eight

A Guide to Peace of Mind and Body

Chip Beardsley

Dedication

This book is dedicated to everyone that has helped and guided me through life.

To my wife and sons that have endured my never-ending ideas and lists with incredible composure and kindness.

To my parents and sister, they must have patience as their superpower for putting up with me.

To my Gilroy family that welcomed me in from the beginning.

To all my friends for helping shape me into who I am today.

This is for all of you.

"The *Optimum Eight* is great for people who want to get into reading. As someone who was never a reader, this book changed that and gave me a sense of guidance for my day to day life."

Lilly Mariscal
High School Senior

"I love this book, succinct and actionable. It contains the blueprint for living a more fulfilling life one day at a time."

Erik Johnson
Business Owner and Entrepreneur

Foreword

The Optimum Eight

People frequently tell me how lucky I am. I think it's true. So many things have worked out for me and I truly enjoy life every day.

When I go to Las Vegas I always hit some kind of jackpot. Small jackpots, but jackpots nonetheless. On the golf course I'm the guy that hits the tree and it bounces back into the fairway.

In real life it has worked out for me as well. I married a beautiful woman who was way out of my league. Not only is she stunning, but she has consistently made me a better person. My two sons are kind, caring human beings that go out of their way to help others. For my career, I lucked into a job that I have loved for 28 years. I really don't know how it worked out so well.

When I sent my first draft of this to my oldest son, he told me I should give everyone a little background information. Don't worry, I will make it quick. I have taught language arts and physical education for 28 years. So as I throw this information your way, it comes from many years working with students that needed a teacher, a coach, a fan, a hype guy or many other different things each day.

As you get into the book you will see that some of my luck has come from being prepared and organized. I have always felt that my best days in class were when I was completely ready to go with a fun, interesting lesson. That goes for my daily life as well. I love having a daily routine and an idea of what I want to accomplish for the day. I'm not talking Groundhog Day here, but structure helps to get the most out of a day. Spontaneity isn't thrown out the window. If I'm out playing volleyball and having a great time, I'm not worrying about making sure I get to my singing or dancing. I am just enjoying the moment. The idea of structure helps us focus on getting to the things we want to achieve or accomplish that day. The beauty of our short list is that it leaves it open for more.

The Optimum Eight is based on practices that have worked for me in my world. Remember that everyone will make adjustments and adaptations that work for their life.

How to Use this Book:

The Optimum Eight was written to be used on a daily basis. It can be read front to back in less than 15 minutes for the first couple of reads and then less than 5 minutes after that.

Please write in this book. Make notes to yourself regarding specific sections. Write down your own list of motivational songs or movies. Have a list of games or workouts that work the best for you. Add to the hacks that can make it easier for you to achieve what you would like each day.

Come back to the book daily to see what you want to do for the day. When you come back and review you can add to your pages.

This book could be used as your guide or reminder to not get lost. Everyone gets busy but we can all take some time out to get to the little things that can make our day better. I look at it like this sometimes. I work out consistently, but it's usually on my own in the garage (weight room). These are some uninspiring workouts at times. So recently I pulled some laundry off of the Peloton and began to use their workouts. This is a million times better. I am actually sweating and working hard. I needed the reminder or the guide to get me going. If you don't have one of those bikes, you can pull free workouts from *YouTube*, *Instagram*, *Pinterest*, and many others.

Make this book your one stop shop to getting your day going. Its sole purpose is to have you think about your day and get living.

What do you want out of your day?

____

____

____

____

____

____

____

____

____

____

____

____

"I say luck is when an opportunity comes along and you're prepared for it."

- Denzel Washington

The Optimum Eight

A Guide to Peace of Mind and Body

by Chip Beardsley

Sometimes when we pick up a book or start to read something we ask ourselves why am I reading this? The answer for most people is they want a better life.

If you've gotten this far you are probably in that group. You are in search of better or improvement.

I am a high school PE teacher and I actually have the ways to improve life as part of the daily routine in my classes. Who knows how to have more fun than a PE teacher? It's my superpower.

So, you aren't crazy for opening this book and it won't be a waste of time, mainly because it won't take too long to read it.

Here is the reality. I know what I am talking about. I wake up daily and consistently enjoy my day. I do it all. I work. I play. I sing. I dance. I care. I learn. And at the end of the day, when my head hits the pillow, you know what I do? I go to sleep. Probably because I know I had a fun, productive day.

I want you to use this book up. Write in it. Highlight areas you want to find quickly. Use the space for notes to add your spin to *The Optimum Eight.*

Let's do this. If you have made it to this point, you are in. You're ready to have something more.

"Start where you are. Use what you have.
Do what you can."
- Arthur Ashe

Before you jump into the book, what are 5 things that you want to do daily?

The Optimum Eight

- Wake up
- Lift/Exercise
- Learn/Read/Listen
- Work
- Inspire
- Play
- Take Responsibility
- Sing/Dance

"Life is like riding a bicycle. To keep your balance, you must keep moving."
- Albert Einstein

"I guess it comes down to a simple choice, really. Get busy living, or get busy dying."
- Andy Dufresne
(*The Shawshank Redemption*)

What would you like to get busy doing?

Wake Up!!!

Get up. You probably slept more than enough. If your alarm goes off it is time to get your day moving. If you set it, there is probably a reason. The sooner you get up, the more time you have to get everything completed.

Yes, sleep is important. We all know this. There are studies all over the world about the benefits of a good night's sleep. What we don't hear about as much is the importance of waking up.

When we wake up when the alarm goes off, we are getting ourselves up on the right foot for success. We are up, ready to go, and starting our day off by doing what we said we were going to do.

Scenario 1 - The alarm goes off, I get out of bed and walk over to the dresser where I placed my phone the night before. I turn the alarm off, pull the covers up so I'm not tempted to climb back in, go downstairs to turn on coffee, and begin my morning routine. Boom! Ready for the day!

Scenario 2 - If we look at this from the opposite side – Alarm goes off, I hit snooze, try to sleep for ten more minutes, hit snooze again, try to close eyes, roll out of bed, and now I'm twenty minutes behind schedule. I'm rushing around, trying to catch up for the time I lost. Maybe I miss my workout or don't get to my yoga. I have to hustle through the rest of the morning and hopefully get to work on time. How does this sound for a start to my day?

The idea of waking up when your alarm goes off tells you that you are ready to get going. I have things that I want to accomplish today so let's get started.

I think back to times when I really popped out of bed ready to go. When I was younger we used to play in Over the Line tournaments on the weekends during the summer. These were all day tournaments on the beach. The only downside to these tournaments was that they would start at 7:00 in the morning. This meant you were waking up at 5:30am on a Saturday. The funny thing was that it was pretty easy to get up and get moving because of the excitement of the day. I call this the Christmas Morning Effect. When we have something to look forward to for the next day it becomes so much easier to jump out of bed and start the day.

When we have a daily mission, we have a reason to wake up. It makes every day Christmas.

Wake up hacks:

- Have your plan for the next day so you know what you are waking up for.
- Put your alarm where you have to get out of bed to turn it off.

Waking Up! Thoughts and Ideas

What helps you wake up in the morning?

How could waking up when the alarm goes off improve your day?

Lift/Exercise

Your body always feels better when you have exercised. You have more energy throughout the day and you feel better about yourself. Find something that you like to do so it doesn't feel like work.

Exercise is a key component to a healthy lifestyle. Oh, is that it? Thanks for the info. It's only the information that everyone in the world says is important.

Get used to it. The information that I'm going to give you isn't mind blowing, earth shattering or "What? No way??!!" It is straightforward, basic, and down to earth.

Yes. You should get up in the morning and do some form of exercise. If you can't do it in the morning, you need to find some time in the day to get moving.

In my mind, it doesn't matter what you want to do for your exercise routine. We can talk about a bunch of different options that you could do for your daily exercise.

Choices:

- Walk
- Jog
- Lift weights
- Ride a bike
- Climb stairs
- Swim
- Surf
- Play a sport
- Yoga

When it comes to doing something that we don't always enjoy, the wording we use can change the way we look at it. When I use the term, "workout", it can make it seem like something you have to do instead of an activity that you get to do. With that in mind, it is better to choose an activity that we enjoy. If we like it, we are more likely to continue and create a habit.

What happens is that when people start an exercise program and they don't really enjoy the activity, it becomes easier to quit. If you don't like running and you choose running as your exercise, then you might be setting yourself up for failure. You need to find an activity that piques your interest enough to keep you coming back for more. It has to grab you, especially in the beginning, so you have time to get in a groove.

For me, I like to play and compete and move and be athletic. I don't love to go out for a 3 mile run. Trust me there are people that enjoy running and swear by it, but it's not necessarily for me. I can go play pickleball for two hours and just get lost in playing. If somebody wants to play 36 holes of golf on the weekend I am in. When I'm at the beach and we are playing volleyball I'm not thinking about when is it going to end. What I mean is that exercise can be different for everyone. You just have to find what works for you.

Daily exercise has so many benefits. You have more energy. You feel better about yourself physically and mentally. And it helps you become prepared to attack the day. Go get after it.

Lift/Exercise Notes

Which exercises or activities will help you get started?

What will be your daily fitness plan?

Who could you get to workout with you?

Learn/Read/Listen

People love to have knowledge. It's nice to know things. It can help for conversations. It can make you more interesting. Things you know can become your ice breakers.

I love to read for knowledge and entertainment. Some books allow me to get lost in another world for a little while, and some give me information to use in my everyday life. I want to be smarter today than I was yesterday.

Listening works just as well in my book. If you aren't a big time reader then listen to audiobooks or podcasts that interest you. It doesn't even have to be so formal. You could just listen to others because people are smart and you can take their ideas and use them to make your life better. You don't even have to pay them. Listening is free!

I can't tell you when I became a reader but it was definitely later in life. I can remember watching my sister devour books as a kid and I couldn't understand what in the world she was doing.

Now I do.

For the most part, I read fiction for entertainment. I want to get lost in another world and create that story in my mind. But as this happens, I tend to connect with the characters and put myself in their shoes. One of my favorites is when Santiago, the main character in Paulo Coelho's *The Alchemist*, starts working at the crystal shop out of necessity. It wasn't a part of his personal mission, not what he was planning to do, but as he starts working there he begins to own the job. He goes out of his way to do his best and make the shop a success. So as I'm connecting with Santiago and his world, I learn that whatever it is that you are doing, make it your mission.

When I'm reading nonfiction though, I am looking to learn. I want to know what super successful people do or have done to get to that point. I love to hear about different ideas and learn how to live life to the fullest. Reading can do all of these things for me.

Listening sometimes seems like it has become a lost art. Many people want to speak so quickly and they want to be heard right away. If you can hold up on trying to speak and be heard all of the time then you can focus your attention on what others are saying. This skill will not only help you in life, but it will also make you a person that others want to speak to. So, when you have that urge to jump in and speak too quickly, stop yourself and wait until they are finished. Trust me.

- Read for fun
- Read to learn
- Learn as much as you can
- Actively listen to people

"Try to learn something about everything and everything about something."
- Thomas Huxley

Learn/Read/Listen Notes

What would you like to learn more about?

Which books would you like to put on your reading list?

Which podcasts could help make your day better?

Work/Be Productive

There is an old saying that goes something like, all work and no play makes someone have a bad day. I would think that the inverse would be true. I love to play and be active, but I know I need balance. I love the feeling of being productive. Maybe working and completing tasks makes the play part of the day more rewarding.

I remember when I first came up with this idea. Wait. No. Actually one of my favorite fellow teachers came up with it and I stole it from her. We taught as a team for a number of years. For those not in the educational world, that means we worked together with combined students to give them the best education possible. Maureen Romac was the teacher I aspired to be. So any time I could take any of her tricks or ideas I was jumping to it. One day I was watching her make a checklist with boxes and I asked her why she was doing that. I mean I looked at the checklist and these were all tasks that I know she completed everyday. So her response was simple, for one, it's a good reminder of the tasks I need to complete for the day. That way nothing gets forgotten. And two, I like the feeling of checking off the box to say, I finished. It seemed kind of funny to me but I decided to give it a shot. Yes, once again she was correct. By using the checklist, I became super efficient and I actually did enjoy checking the boxes. I still do.

I'm not sure if this is inherent in humans, but in my world I see that people generally want to be productive. I believe this because when I see those students and colleagues finish something they have been working on, they light up and glow with feelings of accomplishment.

So once again, if we look at this from the other side, we see how frustrated people become when they aren't getting things done. For me, writing is a good example. When I get going and get some words on a page and send them to my sister to proofread, I feel great. But, when I sit at my computer blankly and think about nothing and everything all at once, I feel like I'm just wasting my time.

Productivity hacks:

- Create a daily checklist of tasks and jobs to complete for the day.
- Always have something you are working on for that day.
- Make a long term checklist of monthly and yearly goals.

"If you spend too much time thinking about a thing, you'll never get it done."
- Bruce Lee

Work/Be Productive

Notes

How do you feel when you complete a task you are working on?

How does it feel when you procrastinate? What can you do to get out of that habit?

To Inspire or Be Inspired-That is the Question

The answer is both. Do things in your everyday life that would inspire others and look to be inspired daily.

I love the feeling of being inspired so I look for ways to get it each day. I can watch a movie, read a book, listen to music, speak to someone that I know is going to make me think, or just plain living.

Movies are great for inspiration. You know I'm right. We all have specific movies that get us going in different ways. For me if I want to get motivated to get more fit I am turning on *Vision Quest* or *Rocky III*. If I want to be inspired on how to be a better person I watch *Ted Lasso*. You can list a couple of your inspirational movies or shows here so you can come back to them.

"Don't count the days, make the days count."
- Muhammad Ali

Movies / Shows

____

____

____

____

____

Yes, I love books. I read all kinds of different genres. I read books and sections of books over and over again because I know how they make me feel. I have read one of my favorites, *How to Win Friends and Influence People* by Dale Carnegie, more than 5 times. I guess I like the way it ignites feelings that make me want to be a better person or one that handles most situations well.

I am 53 years old and if I want to speak to someone that inspires me I tend to call my parents. I don't pick up the phone and say, "Hey, hit me with some inspiration today." I just call and ask questions and I seem to get inspired by their responses. They are completely non-judgmental and straightforward and it seems to put me in the right perspective.

There are so many ways to get you into a mood or out of a mood. Use what works for you. Find your inspiration.

I do address music in Sing/Dance but it is an inspirational game changer. Depending on what you are looking for there is always a song that can get you there. You can see how it works in movies. The right song puts you in a certain mood. It's the same thing in life. When I am a little down about something, I pop on my Reggae Playlist and just like that I'm in a different mood.

Who or what inspires you? Why?

Play!!!

Elementary schools know what they are doing. They teach young people to read and write and think and interact. But they also realize that play should be a big part of the day. It's called recess. I'm not really sure why it doesn't continue into the next levels of school. If we observe people in the world, we see that there is an inherent need for play.

The Play section of our To Do List can also be combined with the Exercise section for some activities. Play can mean so many different things for me. It could mean:

- Golf
- Do the Wordle
- Paddleboard
- Throw a Frisbee
- Play Chess or Cards
- Juggle a soccer ball

I could continue this bulleted list for days because I feel like

I have an Honorary Ph.D. in play.

To play is to do. Let me explain this through my eyes. I have some attention difficulties and major issues with sitting around. While sitting, my legs are always shaking or moving. On vacation I'm not laying out and getting a tan for a couple of reasons. One – I wouldn't tan, I would burn. Two – I could probably lay out for about two minutes and then my legs would start going wild. I have to be doing something.

Because I know this and believe in the idea of play, I prepare myself for these types of situations. In life people are known for certain things about themselves or things they have done. Derek Jeter is known for being the Captain of the Yankees and making that crazy cutoff play against the A's. Robert Frost is known for letting us know that we don't always have to go in the same direction as everyone else because the other way might be better. Muhammad Ali is known for floating like a butterfly and stinging like a bee. Once again I can do this all day.

I, personally, am known for my Activity Bag. Don't worry. I'll explain. Wherever I go (vacations, the beach, the park, work, family functions) I have a bag. This bag has everything. It has a Whiffle bat and balls, a Frisbee, a volleyball, a soccer ball, cards, dice and cups, and more. I know this is very specific, but this is just an example. You would make your bag geared toward your own interests. We would call this bag an emergency kit for boredom. The idea here is to go play something every day. If you prepare yourself, like anything else in life, you will be more apt to follow through.

Play Notes

What will be in your bag?

"It is a happy talent to know how to play."
- Ralph Waldo Emerson

What would be three things that you would like to have on your Play To Do List?

What can you do to make that happen?

Tell about a good play memory that you have.

Take Responsibility

Take responsibility for your actions everyday. Since this is a list of things we can do to make life better, I figured we had to have this one. This action not only makes the day better, but by creating this habit there is no doubt that life will be better.

I was listening to a speaker the other day who was talking about taking responsibility for everything that happens to us. After I heard this I started thinking about all of the excuses we have when something occurs.

Let's take the example of being late for work. I will use this because it happened to me the other day. Here's the background: I'm always early for work. The last couple of weeks they have been doing roadwork on the freeway by my house. So two days last week I got to work a couple of minutes late. Me: "Why are they doing this right now? Why are those cars getting ahead of us in the other lane? Great, I'm gonna be late again because of this." Reality: I knew there was a chance of delay especially because it happened earlier in the week. I could have put my location in maps before I left to get an alternate route. I could have decided to leave a little earlier that week because of the road work. I can take responsibility for my own actions which will help me reduce my frustration in certain situations.

We need to take control of our own lives. The easiest way to do it is to take responsibility for actions. No more excuses.

Don't think you are alone here. I am a major culprit. We have become a culture of blame and excuses. We blame our teachers for our poor grades, we blame our bosses because we dislike our job, we blame our coach, the field, or the referee when we lose a game. I get it. Things don't always work out the way we envision. We all have moments when things don't go our way and we want to blame others or make excuses. I'm not saying we have to be perfect all of the time, but if we can catch ourselves when we get in this mode, we can alleviate a lot of our stress and frustration and keep ourselves out of the excuse zone.

What if we made the decision in our life to never place blame on anyone else, but instead take responsibility for everything that happens to us in our lives. How powerful would that be?

____

____

____

"Character - the willingness to accept responsibility for one's own life - is the source from which self-respect springs."
-Joan Didion

Take Responsibility Notes

What can you do to take ownership of your day? Use a specific example.

Sing and Dance

Sing and dance like nobody is watching or listening.

Music, for me, is a game changer. It's the mood creator. You know this. To get pumped up to do a workout, you pick a specific playlist of songs that are upbeat and fast. When you want to get out of a funk where you are feeling down, you can throw on a playlist that will lift your spirits.

As we go back to the idea of being prepared, we know that we have to have these songs cued up on a list. I have a variety of playlists that I use for all kinds of different situations. There is a scene in *The Internship* where they have a "Get Psyched Playlist." We should all have these lists ready to go. In baseball they have these songs that players use for their walk-up songs. These are parts of tunes that get the player in the best mindset for his at bat. We should have our own walk-up songs close at hand. What are yours?

"There are shortcuts to happiness, and dancing is one of them."
- Vicky Baum

Your Walk-up Songs

____

____

____

____

____

____

____

When we get these songs going it's time to sing and dance. One of the best places to make this happen is in the good old automobile. I know I do a lot of my best singing and dancing in the car. I crank up the volume so my voice doesn't mess up the sound too much and then get moving. I feel like the steering wheel helps out my groove and not being able to stand probably makes my dance style a little better.

Sing/Dance Notes

Where do you groove?

Final Thoughts

The Optimum Eight means when I get to these then I am probably winning the day. I want to feel good about how the day went before I go to sleep. Winning the day by using these strategies gives me a better chance at owning my life. If I can win today, then I have a better chance of dominating the next one. It's like starting a streak and then working to keep it going.

What is it going to take for you to win each day?

____

____

____

____

____

"Either you run the day or the day runs you."
-Jim Rohn

You may wonder, how do we win every day? Is it even possible? The answer is that if we can do a lot of these activities in a day we are giving ourselves a shot. A day doesn't have to be perfect to be a win. There are days where I feel like I crushed it and won 10-0. Other days could be a close one, like 5-4. It still equals a win.

Throughout the day, I think about how everything is going. I'll make a call to my wife after my first classes and she will ask me if I'm winning. Sometimes I tell her I am crushing it or I might tell her that I need to make a comeback. It doesn't bother me if I am down because I can do more later in the day to get back into the win column. Somedays might not feel like a win, but each day I can make the effort to get better.

The Optimum Eight is about you getting the most out of your day, which will lead you to getting the most out of your life.

How will you win the day and create the life you want?

____

____

____

____

____

The Optimum Eight

- ☐ Wake up
- ☐ Lift/Exercise
- ☐ Learn/Read/Listen
- ☐ Work
- ☐ Inspire
- ☐ Play
- ☐ Take Responsibility
- ☐ Sing Dance
- ☐
- ☐
- ☐
- ☐

The Optimum Eight

- [ ] Wake up
- [ ] Lift/Exercise
- [ ] Learn/Read/Listen
- [ ] Work
- [ ] Inspire
- [ ] Play
- [ ] Take Responsibility
- [ ] Sing Dance
- [ ]
- [ ]
- [ ]
- [ ]

The Optimum Eight

- ☐ Wake up
- ☐ Lift/Exercise
- ☐ Learn/Read/Listen
- ☐ Work
- ☐ Inspire
- ☐ Play
- ☐ Take Responsibility
- ☐ Sing Dance
- ☐
- ☐
- ☐
- ☐

The Optimum Eight

- ☐ Wake up
- ☐ Lift/Exercise
- ☐ Learn/Read/Listen
- ☐ Work
- ☐ Inspire
- ☐ Play
- ☐ Take Responsibility
- ☐ Sing Dance
- ☐
- ☐
- ☐
- ☐

The Optimum Eight

- [ ] Wake up
- [ ] Lift/Exercise
- [ ] Learn/Read/Listen
- [ ] Work
- [ ] Inspire
- [ ] Play
- [ ] Take Responsibility
- [ ] Sing Dance
- [ ]
- [ ]
- [ ]
- [ ]

The Optimum Eight

- [ ] Wake up
- [ ] Lift/Exercise
- [ ] Learn/Read/Listen
- [ ] Work
- [ ] Inspire
- [ ] Play
- [ ] Take Responsibility
- [ ] Sing Dance
- [ ]
- [ ]
- [ ]
- [ ]

The Optimum Eight

- [ ] Wake up
- [ ] Lift/Exercise
- [ ] Learn/Read/Listen
- [ ] Work
- [ ] Inspire
- [ ] Play
- [ ] Take Responsibility
- [ ] Sing Dance
- [ ]
- [ ]
- [ ]
- [ ]

Made in the USA
Middletown, DE
19 September 2024

60727315R00046